He did this so that all the peoples of the earth might know that the hand of the Lord is powerful and so that you might always fear the Lord your God.

Joshua 4:24

He did this so that all the peoples of the earth might

that **the hand of the Lord is** p

and so that you might always fear the Lord you

Joshua 4:24

# Nine Charles Street

*remembering the power of the Lord*

BY HANNE LARSON

## ACKNOWLEDGMENTS

Thank you Leslea for being used by God to remind me why I was
writing this book in the first place and what this is all about.
Thanks to you Barb for your enthusiasm and excitement about this book.
Your ideas and creativity were such a gift.
Scott, you not only cheered me on from the sidelines, but you sacrificially did
the dirty work of the edits. A true act of love. I love you!!

"Nine Charles Street" © 2006 Hanne Larson. All rights reserved.
No part of this publication may be reproduced in any form or by any means -
electronic, mechanical, photocopying, recording or otherwise - without the prior written permission of the
publisher.
Graphic design by Julie Anderson
Published in Gainesville, Georgia, by
Praxis Press, Inc.
3630 Thompson Bridge Rd., Suite #15-100
Gainesville, GA 30506
www.praxispublishing.com
Unless otherwise indicated, all Scripture quotations are taken from the Holy Bible, New Living Translation,
copyright ©1996. Used by permission of Tyndale House Publishers, Inc., Wheaton, Illinois 60189. All rights
reserved.
When (NIV) is indicated: Scripture taken from the HOLY BIBLE, NEW INTERNATIONAL VERSION
©1972, 1978, 1984 by International Bible Society. Used by permission of Zondervan. All rights reserved.

To Order Additional Copies Of Nine Charles Street
go to www.PraxisPublishing.com

Printed in the United States of America.
ISBN-13: 978-0-9754305-5-2
ISBN-10: 0-9754305-5-6

# Dedication

To my parents,
Henry and Minnie Eskelund,
who in living out their faith
have passed it on to me.

To my children, Sarah and David,
that they too will know that
the hand of the Lord is powerful.

# CONTENTS

9

He did this so that
all the peoples of the earth
might know that
the hand of the Lord
is powerful
and so that you might always
fear the Lord your God.

(Joshua 4:24 NLT)

# PREFACE

In April 2003, the Lord met us in a powerful way during the last day of our Straight Ahead Ministries National Conference. Scott and I went away from that conference with a commitment to seek the Lord in a fresh way and to be open to anything He would speak to us concerning us and the future of the ministry.

Scott was able to go away for a few days to commit the time to prayer, while I committed to pray and seek God during the day while the kids were in school. On one of those days, while going over Bible passages the Lord had given us at the conference, the Lord spoke to me about this book.

I recalled how Joshua was told by the Lord to put down twelve stones as a memorial to future generations. I felt that the Lord was asking us to document what His powerful hand had done for nine years at our aftercare home for kids transitioning out of juvenile lock-up on 9 Charles Street in Westboro, Massachusetts. It seemed important to do this before moving on to the big task ahead of opening Straight Ahead Academy.

I immediately called Scott on his cell phone.

"Scott I have a message for you from the Lord. You are supposed to write a book on 9 Charles Street so that what He did there will be remembered in future generations."

A couple of months went by, and we didn't talk about the book. During this time, I felt challenged to take a look at how fear of failure has influenced my life and took some time to think about that and talk it through with God. As I was praying and journaling, I asked the Lord to show me how fear holds me back from what He has for me.

The first thing I wrote down was "I won't even consider that I would be the one to write the book." The minute I wrote that on paper, I had to respond with a willingness to consider that He just might have spoken that to me, and not to Scott.

So here I am, after much prayer and soul searching. I'm saying "yes" to writing a memorial to what God has done at 9 Charles Street so that "people might know that the Lord is powerful and so that you might always fear the Lord your God."

Those who sow
in tears

will reap
with songs of joy.

Psalm 126:5 (NIV)

# A DREAM
## FROM DESPAIR

# TEARS FOR THOMAS

It was the summer of 1989. I had been leading a Bible study at Westboro Detention Center in Massachusetts for two years, and Scott had recently started going in with me as my partner. It was great going in together, not only for the support but also for the gift to develop relationships with these teenage boys together and to share experiences with each other as we drove home each week.

Over those two years, we had seen many guys respond to God's love and develop a real desire to change their lives and go in a different direction. One of these boys was Thomas.

We both connected with Thomas quickly. He had a pleasant personality and was extremely likeable. He was one of those kids who wasn't just sorry that he had gotten caught, but was truly saddened by the choices he had made. One

night after Bible study, he wanted to stay back to talk to us.

Thomas said that he was really scared to get released. He explained that he was a member of a gang, and that if he went back home, he was pretty sure he wouldn't make it.

"What is it that you think you need, Thomas?" we asked.

He said that his desire was to go to a place where he could grow in his faith and be part of a family. "Isn't there a place like that?" he asked. We promised Thomas that we would try to find such a place for him.

Driving home, we talked about how important it would be to find him a place. I was so glad Scott was with me and that he was in the loop on this. He is one of the most resourceful people I know. He seems to always be able to connect with just the right people at just the right time, so I was pretty confident that Thomas would be taken care of.

As the week went on, and we were praying for the Lord to give us new ideas and open doors, we got more and more discouraged. Most Christian programs we called had policies against taking anyone under the age of 18. Thomas was 16. The programs for kids under 18 required heavy involvement from parents, which wasn't possible for Thomas.

We couldn't believe it! We had to go back the following week and tell Thomas there wasn't any place for him after release.

A couple of weeks later, Thomas was released. The last night we saw him at Bible study, we assured him we would be praying for him. We also gave him our phone number and told him we would help any way we could.

A few weeks later, when we got off the elevator at the detention center, one of the staff met us and asked, "Did you read about Thomas in the Boston Globe?" "No," we hadn't read anything about him in the paper. We were told that he had been found in an alley castrated and stabbed in the neck by a rival gang.

Thomas was dead! We were shocked. Here was a kid who really wanted to turn his life around, and he didn't get the chance. We felt angry, frustrated, sad, and confused. It just couldn't be right that God didn't have a place for him and so many others who were ready for a new start.

Scott and I went home and talked a lot. We started talking to God about it too, letting Him in on this big problem we had "discovered."

Didn't He care about this? Couldn't He raise up a place for guys like Thomas where, like he had said, they could grow in their faith and live as a family? We started pleading with God for this.

As a result of talking to God about this, we started to sense that He was putting it back to us. We sensed that it was His heart's desire to have a place for these guys to go to, and that He wanted to use us to be a part of making this possible.

Once we really felt that God was asking us to open up an aftercare discipleship home for kids, Scott was off and running. A big challenge is always a great motivator for Scott. I was also getting pretty excited about the prospect of bringing these boys home to live with us. At that stage I believed that if only I could take them home and love them, everything would turn out great. Sometimes it is good to be naïve.

So, in our October 1989 newsletter, we shared with our prayer partners and supporters what we felt the Lord had put on our hearts. We asked them to pray with us for direction and for God's provision.

A few busy months went by with Scott contacting individuals and foundations to raise money to purchase a home. It seemed almost impossible to us that absolutely no one responded. How could this be? It had seemed so clear to us that the Lord was asking us to do this. Had we not heard Him right?

*You brought us to a place of great abundance...*

(Psalm 66:12, NLT)

# A PLACE
## OF ABUNDANCE

# GREG'S BONUS

As we were starting to feel reconciled to the fact that God wasn't having us open up a home for released juvenile offenders, we felt tapped on the shoulder by the Lord. It came in the form of a challenge that we believed came directly from Him.

Didn't we have some money in savings that Scott had put aside when he was a stockbroker? At first it was difficult for Scott to consider giving that up, but as we talked it through, it became clear that this is what God was asking of us. (Our board later made this into an interest-free loan).

No more money came in that fall towards the home, but we were feeling confident that the Lord's hand was in it. In January, we received a letter from a college friend of mine.

Greg wrote that he had received our October letter talking about our desire to open a discipleship home. As he read that letter, he felt the Lord impressing on his heart to give his bonus from work that year toward the start up of this home. Not only did the Lord ask him to do this, but He also told him the specific amount of money that it would be. Greg only told his dad and his girlfriend about this. He said that this became his motivation at work and that his bonus became the amount the Lord had said. "So, enclosed you will find a check for $50,000."

At the time, Scott and I lived in a small one-bedroom apartment at our church. I can still remember the two of us standing in our tiny kitchen reading this letter, then embracing as tears rolled down our cheeks. Our initial feelings were fear and awe. We realized this endeavor was so much bigger than us and that it was going to

be pulled off by Almighty God!

That sent us house hunting! Could we buy a house for $50,000 and the additional $40,000 we had put in? Absolutely not, but we were confident that more would come.

*We realized this endeavor was so much bigger than us and that it was going to be pulled off by almighty God.*

# THE NINETEEN-ROOM VICTORIAN

What did we need? We needed a big house with lots of bedrooms. We knew a Christian realtor who had been supporting our ministry since the beginning. He took us around and showed us many old houses, always praying with us that the Lord would show us just the right thing.

We had given him a price range that we thought realistic. There were many old houses around with lots of rooms, but no large living areas in them. And, most of what we looked at needed so much work. We were starting to get overwhelmed and discouraged.

My parents, missionaries in Denmark, came for a visit that summer of 1990. We thought it would be fun to take them around with us to explore some house possibilities. In a couple of weeks, they climbed many stairs with us, looked at many properties that were falling apart, and heard many "If we could just change this or that" from us.

One afternoon, after seeing a couple of houses, we went to a park for our afternoon coffee. My parents shared with us their concern. "We really think you are looking at the wrong houses," they said. "It seems that you are looking for what you think God can afford rather that what is really needed."

When they stated that, Scott remembered being told about a beautiful house in Westboro that a church had looked at to buy. It wasn't what the church needed, but they had said it would be an amazing house for an aftercare home. We hadn't pursued it, since the price tag was way too high. But with this new perspective from my parents, we decided to drive by to see if it was still for sale.

Oh my, we could hardly believe it! The house was beautiful and very large. It looked amazing to us. It was beyond what we could think or imagine. There was no "For Sale" sign though, so we drove by.

Then Scott stopped the car and said, "Maybe I should go knock on the door and see if they still want to sell it." That's Scott for you. Never take "no" for an answer. As I was cringing in the car at Scott's boldness, I think my parents were praying. Anyway, Scott came back and told us to come. The owners were home and wanted to show us the house.

It turned out they had just taken it off the market, but actually still wanted to sell it. As we walked through each room of this 6,000-square-foot Victorian house with its 19 rooms and 5 bathrooms, we were overwhelmed. It was a historic home built a hundred years ago by a well-known admiral, and had been immaculately preserved. Was it possible that the Lord had this for us? It almost seemed too good even for the Lord to provide.

Scott explained to the owner what we were planning. He seemed excited and said he would be willing to work with us so that this could happen. When he asked about our financial situation, we said we had $90,000 and that we needed to end up with a very low monthly mortgage payment. He laughed.

We went away praying. My parents agreed that this really did seem to be the house for us.

By the end of the summer, no more money had come in. We got together with our board for an all-day prayer meeting. We continued to tell the Lord we were willing to give up the whole idea if this was not of Him. By the end of the day it felt more confirmed to us that it was in fact what the Lord was doing.

*It was beyond what we could think or imagine.*

21

# SOME MINNESOTA FRIENDS

In the early fall, we got a phone call from some Minnesota friends. Paul and Linda were in Boston for some meetings Paul was attending for orthopedic surgeons. They wondered if we could meet them for lunch in Cambridge with another couple there for the meetings. We had the afternoon open so we drove in to meet them.

On the way, we discussed whether we should ask Paul and Linda to consider giving towards the purchase of this house. They had been very generous to us and the ministry in the past, so maybe this would be a good opportunity. We prayed about it and asked the Lord to make it perfectly clear to us if we were to mention anything. Otherwise we were committed to

letting it go.

We had an enjoyable lunch with them and their friends, Dick and Joy. They asked all about the ministry and about our vision for the discipleship home, but money never came up. As we were walking out, we looked at each other. Did we just miss a great opportunity? We quickly agreed that we had not been given the go-ahead to ask. "Lord, this is your deal; we leave it with you."

A couple of months later, I was in Minnesota attending a shower for my good friend Sue, hosted by Paul and Linda. Paul was walking around with trays of food serving us. When he came to me, he said, "Oh I meant to tell you what happened after we had lunch

*Did we just miss a great opportunity?*

together in Cambridge." He told me that he and Linda had told Dick and Joy that if they would give $25,000 to Straight Ahead they would do the same. Then they would also give $25,000 to a charity selected by Dick and Joy. "So you should be getting a check in the mail for $50,000 soon."

Is God unbelievable or what?

# AN AFFORDABLE LOAN

Now, all we needed was a loan with a low interest rate, and we would be all set.

Someone told us about a Christian foundation that provided low-rate loans to Christian non-profits. We got really excited as we started seeing our impossible dream becoming a reality. We had pretty much been given a green light, so it was just a matter of going through the process. Scott completed the required applications and paperwork.

When we left in December to spend Christmas with family in Minnesota, we anticipated getting notification of loan approval while we were away. We got a phone call from Kathy, who worked with us in the ministry. We were so excited. I stood near the phone while Scott was talking, getting ready to celebrate as soon as he hung up.

Then, my heart sank as I watched Scott's face. All he said was, "The loan fell through." We couldn't believe it. This had seemed like such a sure thing and like such a provision from the Lord. "What's going on?" We went to bed that night pretty down. We couldn't believe that God had brought us this far just to drop the ball like that. "Now what, Lord?"

The next day we got another phone call from Kathy. "You will never believe what just came in the mail." An anonymous gift had come in for $25,000. Wow, the Lord did even better than the best we could imagine!!

By this time, we had been talking to the owner about buying this house for about six months. He was starting to get anxious about getting something finalized. Scott met with him to suggest he lower the price even further, but that pushed him over the edge, and as a result he kicked Scott out of the house.

We went home and prayed, for it was clear that the owner was no longer willing to work with us. We asked people to pray for the Lord to intervene, soften this man's heart, and show us what to do next, if anything.

A few weeks later, Scott phoned the owner and asked him to go out for breakfast with us. he agreed. We explained how a significant amount of the money had been donated, that we still needed $110,000, but were unable to get a loan at an interest rate that allowed us to afford the monthly payments.

"How about if I provide the financing?" He offered. We then discussed what that might look like. We ended up with a $50,000 loan at zero percent interest and a $60,000 loan at 5 percent. We moved in with a $500 monthly house payment. Only the Lord could have orchestrated all of this.

On July 3, 1991, we moved into 9 Charles Street, Westboro, Massachusetts. Truly a gift from God.

*Only the Lord could have orchestrated all of this.*

Look at the lilies and how they grow

(Matthew 6:28 NLT)

# DOWN
## TO THE DETAILS

# WALLPAPER & FURNITURE

A 6,000 square foot beautiful Victorian home needed a little more furniture than we had in our one bedroom apartment. How in the world would this happen?

We would need a dining room table and chairs for at least 12 people. Scott and I picked up newspapers and started hunting through ads. Wow, large dining room sets were not cheap. We came across one ad that read, "Large oversized trestle table with 2 benches, $250." That sounded interesting, so we phoned and went to see it.

The owner apologized, saying it was probably too big and a little beat up. Her husband had used it as a worktable in his workshop. It was full of hammer marks and nail holes. We took one look and realized it was more than perfect. The two benches were big enough for at least five people each, and there would be plenty of room for two chairs on each end. Scott offered $75 for the set. The owner said, "Sure, we just really want it out of here."

After a good sanding and finishing, it was absolutely beautiful. This table became the centerpiece of the home, a daily reminder of God's faithfulness and provision for us.

With the attractive table in the dining room, we needed to do something with the walls. We wanted beautiful wallpaper to give this room a really homey look. With such a large room and high ceilings, that could get costly. I decided to keep my eyes open.

We did a lot of our shopping at a building surplus store. One day, I saw a bin of wallpaper that caught my eye, a beautiful burgundy that would be perfect. All they had was in this bin, and I wasn't sure if it would be enough. I thought it must be the right amount because it was just the right thing for our dining room. So I bought it all for $12.50.

I couldn't wait to get home to put it up. I have to admit I was getting a little nervous as each roll was used up. I ended up with one small piece left over, just five inches by eight inches. Unbelievable! We thanked the Lord for His good taste and ability to figure out wallpaper measurements.

The living room was huge - by far the largest room in the house, with two beautiful crystal chandeliers hanging from the 10-foot ceiling. We definitely needed to do something with the walls. After painting them, we realized something else was needed to complete the room.

A few days later, at a wallpaper store, I saw a clearance bin with really wide Victorian borders, exactly the amount we needed for the living room. Usually, these wide borders are quite expensive, so I asked about the price. The clerk said, "You can take all of them for $10."

The borders were perfect and were, of course, the perfect match for the paint we had already applied.

Another challenge: How to furnish this huge living room with furniture that would fit its style, yet be sturdy enough to accommodate rough-and-tumble teenage boys.

We were praying that the Lord would show us just the right thing as we once again looked at newspaper ads. But, only a few things seemed even worth looking at.

One day on my way to something else, I decided to stop at a furniture store. Of course, we had not considered buying new furniture. But for some reason I felt a strong urge to stop.

I knew they had some clearance items in a back room. So I headed straight there.

Wow! In the clearance room was a large blue sectional couch that would fit perfectly in the living room. I was so excited. I couldn't wait to see the price. It was marked down to half price. The original price was $3,399, and now it was marked down to $1,549. I was so disappointed. This really was the perfect furniture, but too much money.

As I was walking away, a young man came running after me. He said that the manager had just told him to put a "damaged" sticker on the sectional because of a missing screw. Now the price was $309.80.

This furniture became known as the miracle couch. And it lived up to its name, for many of God's transforming miracles occurred as guys were sitting on that very couch.

# REGULAR SIZE CEREAL BOWLS, PLEASE

Before we started our aftercare home, I had never experienced 16- to18-year-old boys' eating habits and appetites. I was shocked and a bit concerned. The grocery bills were getting huge, and I was afraid that there was no way we could continue affording them. One of our biggest expenses was cereal. These guys didn't eat cereal out of cereal bowls; they ate it from large mixing bowls!

Scott and I decided to have a talk with the guys about this. We said, "You guys just can't eat this much cereal. We are going to have to limit it. Grocery bills are way too high, and a big part of it is cereal." The boys sadly agreed to cut back and start using the regular cereal bowls.

The next day we received a letter from the Worcester Food Bank saying we had been approved to shop there. We went right away. I never saw so much cereal in my life--so many varieties, and the cost was 13 cents per pound.

Unbelievable…or was it?

Unbelievable...

or was it?

# GOD'S HANDPICKED DOG

Wouldn't it be great to have a dog?

We talked to the guys about it, and all agreed this was something we needed in the house.

What kind should we get? Definitely a big one. How about a black lab? Not a brand new puppy though. It should be trained.

The next morning I told Scott I would pick up the neighborhood paper when I went out. Maybe there would be some dogs

advertised in it.

Scanning the ads, I thought, "What could we afford? Not much. Wow. Black labs are expensive. It wasn't looking good. Oh wait a minute here is one - 1 1/2 year-old black lab mix looking for a loving home, call…"

I phoned and learned the dog was free to a good home. We were so excited.

Scott and I jumped in the car to pick her up. "What do you want to name her?" he asked.

"We can't name her - she's a year and a half old. She has a

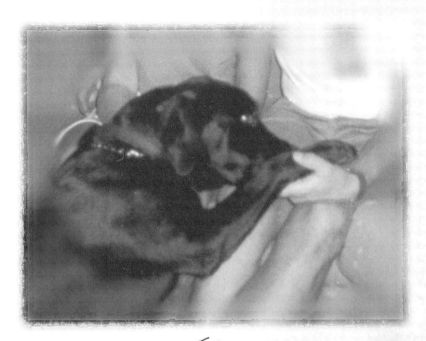

name."

"Well what would you want to name her if you could?"

"Oh... I think Sammy."

When we got there, the owner invited us to follow her into the back yard." As we did, she called out, "Come here, Sammy!"

Thank you, God, for the dog you hand-picked for us.

*Thank you, God, for the dog you handpicked for us.*

He will give you
all you need

from day to day.

Matthew 6:33 (NLT)

# ALL
## I NEED

# I AM WEAK,
# HE IS STRONG

We had been in the house about three months when our second boy, Sean, came. He had been in the very first Bible study I conducted in a detention center in Massachusetts four years earlier. At the study, he was bouncing off the walls. He was one of those kids I almost wished hadn't come, he was so disruptive.

After that first week's study, Sean had been transferred to a different unit. A month later, he was back in the study. I almost didn't recognize him. Knowing that he had a twin brother, I thought maybe this was Sean's twin. He greeted me extremely politely, and I hesitantly said, "S..e..a..n?"

"Yes. It is me," he replied. He sat down calmly, opened his Bible and eagerly participated in the group. I was shocked. I couldn't figure out

how this could be the same Sean.

After the study, I asked what had happened. He said that he had given his life to Jesus and that he felt like a new person inside. The staff even commented afterwards, "He is just not the same kid."

Now, four years later we had reconnected, and we were excited about what God had in store for Sean's life.

Sean struggled greatly the two weeks he was with us. One night he told us, "I would feel more comfortable if you would beat me rather than love me." The next day he ran.

That was a dark morning for us. We were back to one boy and losing hope. It didn't seem like God was doing much here. As I walked into the office later, Scott said, "I forgot to tell you, but we are supposed to speak at a couple's banquet tonight."

My mouth dropped open in shock. "You'll have to do it, I have nothing to say."

"No, they specifically said they wanted both of us to speak."

I walked into the living room, plopped down into the big blue recliner, and cried. Not only was God not doing anything here, but now we had to stand up in front of people and talk about it. I felt empty and full of anxiety and dread.

I'm not sure how long I sat there and cried. But I do know I felt impressed to get my Bible and look up Hebrews chapter 4.

"God's promise of entering his place of rest still stands…only we who believe can enter his place of rest" (vs.1-3).

In that blue chair, God took me on a journey, way back to when He first called me to this ministry in 1979, my junior year in college. He reminded me of how certain I was of His call and how time and time again, He had met me when things seemed beyond what I could

bear.

The journey was full of stories of stepping out, believing Him, seeing His faithfulness, and experiencing His rest. Now, He was inviting me once again to believe Him and enter His rest, a place of safety and peace. I felt as if I could have stayed in that chair forever. Especially if I didn't have to go speak!

Instead He gave me the opportunity to share those stories of His amazing faithfulness to me through the years. From feeling empty and having nothing to say, He had so filled me, my cup was overflowing.

*He had met me when things seemed beyond what I could bear.*

# ALWAYS ENOUGH

After we had been been in the home for 3 1/2 years, Scott and I had our first child, Sarah. Fifteen months later, we had David. When they were babies, I often felt totally spent, especially when Scott was speaking at weekend retreats.

We had created a tradition of having a big Sunday dinner after church--a time when we could all sit down together and connect. Sometimes, friends of the guys would join us too. Usually, we all enjoyed this time, yet sometimes, it was quite a disappointment.

One particular Sunday stands out to me. Scott was away. I had gotten up early and put dinner into the oven, setting the timer for it to bake while we were at church. There were seven boys living with us at that time.

After getting the babies ready and running upstairs several times for wake-up calls to the guys, we finally got out the door. Some straggled into church a little late since they were now driving their own cars.

Dinner after church was a downer. A couple of guys had stopped at McDonalds on the way home and weren't hungry. One of our rules was that everyone had to sit together and eat. Naturally, attitudes were less than great. No one seemed to like the dinner, the babies were cranky, and I had had it.

When dinner was over, I retreated to our

"private" living room, closed the door and hoped no one would ever open it again. I would have been happy if I never had to see another ungrateful adolescent boy as long as I lived.

I was trying to "escape" by reading my Better Homes and Gardens magazine when Moe walked in. "Do you think we could talk?" All my insides were saying, "Absolutely not!!" But somehow the words that came out were, "Sit down".

The most amazing thing happened. Moe, who had lived

with us for more than two years, opened up about his struggles and journey with God in a way he never had done before. As we talked God's presence was powerfully at work, and we got to encounter Him. The renewing of my spirit and emotional energy was amazing. By the time we finished talking, I had received from God more than I could have gotten from a quiet "escape" with my magazine. Oh, how He knew what I needed most.

*As we talked God's presence was powerfully at work...*

# MORE THAN I COULD ASK

Scott had been offered a two-week, all-expenses-paid fishing trip to Alaska. It was a "no brainer" that, of course, he should go. We had seven guys in the house, and Sarah and David, who were two and one at the time. As I look back, those two weeks stand out as some of the hardest I had in the house.

When Scott returned, I was more than exhausted and desperately looking forward to a break. Scott had told me that the day after his return would be mine to do whatever I wanted. He would be there for the guys and take care of our children. That was the carrot that kept me going for the last few days of Scott's trip.

The day Scott returned, he told me that he had just received a phone call from the dentist.

"Tomorrow is the only day he can take me for my big procedure."

My heart sank. I had the whole day planned. For days, it was what I had been looking forward to. All I wanted was one day to myself. Was that too much to ask?

I responded in disbelief saying, "All I need is…" Then, the phone rang. I couldn't believe Scott answered it, "It's for you. It's Bev." Bev was a friend from Nashville I didn't see or hear from very often. I didn't think I had it in me to be "up" for the phone call.

"Hi, Bev."

"Hi, Hanne, I know this is really short notice, but my friend and I are coming up this weekend to stay at the Four Seasons Hotel in

Boston. We have all expenses paid and wondered if you would want to join us?

I could not believe what the Lord provided in response to my heart's cry, "All I need is…" My thoughts and plans were way smaller than the Four Seasons in Boston for a weekend.

Thank you Lord for providing abundantly above what I could ask or imagine.

*I couldn't believe what the Lord provided in response to my heart's cry...*

God is
building you as
living stones...

*(1 Peter 2:5, NLT)*

# LIVING
## STONES

# JOHNNY TRANSFORMED

I told Scott, "I think I'm going to have a hard time liking Johnny. I could tell that this former gang leader was used to bossing people around. Now, he thought he could do that here, including telling me how to cook. In my estimation, he was ungrateful and arrogant. In fact he said, "Three things I never say are: Please, thank-you, and I'm sorry."

That statement got us off to a bad start, but somehow I did believe God had sent him to us and that God had started a work in Johnny that He was going to finish.

Johnny had been locked up several times before, but this last time had been different for him. For the first time in his life, he began taking a serious look at where he was headed. That reality drew him in desperation to God.

When he attended our weekly Bible study in the detention center, Scott and I had seen a spiritual hunger. This hunger, combined with his desperation, gave him the power to choose to come to our discipleship home, rather than returning to what he was accustomed to. Johnny knew why he had come to our home, no matter how rough around the edges he was.

Scott and I got to witness first hand what God can do with a desperate heart. Johnny not only became a strong leader in our home, but also became a leader in the community.

His hunger for God drove him to get involved in as many church youth groups as possible. At one point, he was attending four each week. Because of Johnny's leadership, the rest of the guys in the house went too.

We also started a weekly Bible study at the house that was open for guys to bring friends to.

to Bible college, he had gone on three mission trips: one to Haiti, one to the Dominican Republic, and one to Mexico.

A transformation had taken place in a desperate heart, and by the way, Johnny got really good at saying, "Please, thank-you, and I'm sorry".

*A transformation had taken place in a desperate heart...*

With Johnny's influence, about 30 kids showed up each week.

At the grocery store where he worked, Johnny got to be known as the "singing broom pusher." The football coach at his high school started apologizing each time he caught himself swearing.

By the time Johnny was ready to move on

# JAY SET FREE

Jay was the first guy who came to us who did not come straight out of lock-up. Johnny was his brother. Although Jay was older, he had always looked up to his gang leader brother. Jay had also been involved in this gang.

When Johnny called to invite Jay to spend Thanksgiving with him at our home, Jay was quite leery. I remember meeting Jay the first time. He never looked up and hardly said anything. When he did speak, he stuttered so badly that it was difficult to understand him. Most of the time, he would just sit and look down.

Although Jay was 20 years old, he was doing nothing with his life other than drugs. He hadn't been in school since eighth grade and had never had a job. He had been diagnosed with an eye impairment that left him legally blind. It seemed that Jay was filled with a lot of sadness and little

hope. We were so glad that he had decided to come see Johnny play football after Thanksgiving dinner and stay with us for the weekend.

That Friday night, Scott was speaking at a large youth event where Johnny was sharing his story of what God had done in his life. At the end of the night Jay surrendered his life to Jesus.

On Sunday, Johnny asked us if Jay could stay a little longer.

We sat down with Jay and asked him to tell us what he really wanted. It took a lot of effort for him to express what he was feeling inside. Yet, it became clear to us that Jay desperately wanted a new start and was looking for an opportunity to grow in his brand new faith. We saw hope in his eyes that we had not seen before.

happened. I picked up the boys from a church youth group they had attended. Everyone piled into the car and started talking about what had happened that night. Jay was the most eager.

All of a sudden it hit me, Jay was not stuttering one bit. He was talking confidently, which I had never heard him do before. "Jay, are you hearing yourself talk?" I asked. "You are not stuttering anymore!"

"I know," he said. "Every time I talk about the Lord or am praying, I don't stutter!"

The transformation was amazing. The following fall, Jay went to Bible college - and the miracles go on and on.

*We saw hope*
*in his eyes*
*that we had*
*not seen before.*

We told Jay that to stay in our home, he would have to enroll in school and get a job. Both of these were very threatening things for Jay. Because of his age, we enrolled him in a GED program where he became a model student. Jay had to work extra hard with his limited eyesight, but he gave it his all.

He also got a job at the local grocery store and did amazingly well at his first-ever job.

After a few weeks, a most amazing thing

# ANDRE CREATED FOR A PURPOSE

One of the highlights for us was taking the guys on mission trips during the summer. It was such a privilege to serve alongside them and see how much they were willing to give of themselves. It was often a time when passion was ignited in their hearts for something bigger that God had for their lives.

It was very disappointing to us when Andre dug in his heels and refused to sign up for the mission trip because it involved a plane ride.

Despite our efforts in presenting this idea in various ways, he was stubbornly firm in his decision. Not only were we sad that he would miss the trip but also for the opportunity he would miss seeing God working through him.

We started praying that the Lord would come up with another creative idea for Andre. Let me tell you, it is never a stretch for the Lord to get creative. It is His very nature!

We had heard about a possibility for Andre. A Christian camp in New Hampshire was running a week long camp for disabled adults and needed personal care providers. Andre said he was willing to give it a try.

Off he went to a week of being assigned to one disabled man the entire time. They would be together for everything - eating sleeping, recreation, and whatever else was planned.

We waved Andre off with a bit of anxiety, hoping and praying that this was a good thing.

*...I finally know what I was created for.*

Half way through the week, we received a phone call from Andre. We were eager to find out how things were going. Was he looking for us to come pick him up? What would he say? I stood next to Scott trying to listen in on what he was saying.

"Scott, now I finally know what I was created for."

He did this so that
all the peoples of
the earth might know that
the hand of the
Lord is powerful
and so that you might always
fear the Lord your God.

(Joshua 4:24)

# EPILOGUE

These are mere glimpses of our nine years at 9 Charles Street. Volumes could be written on our journey, as well as those of each of the 35 or so guys who came in and out of our home during those years.

So much pain. So much joy. So much disappointment. So much celebration. So much failure. So much victory. The stories go on and on.

What was constant was the presence of the Lord and the amazing way He showed Himself to each of us.

We truly got to taste and see that the Lord is good, and that His hand is powerful.

When Joshua was asked by the Lord to build a memorial to Him so that future generations might know that the hand of the Lord is powerful, he was still on the journey.

In a similar way God has prompted me to record what He has done at this particular time. Our home on 9 Charles Street was sold, but our journey continues.

Having just opened Straight Ahead Academy, a home and school where boys can grow in faith and character, we are standing at the threshold of the new things God has ahead.

As I reflect and remember how God so mightily worked at 9 Charles Street, I am overwhelmed with gratitude and an awareness of His invitation to continue to trust in His presence and provision.

My prayer is that this book will be a memorial to the Lord and an inspiration to move on into new territories where only His powerful hand can sustain us.

*...I am overwhelmed with gratitude and an awareness of His invitation to continue to trust in His presence and provision.*

## PHOTO CREDITS:

...eoples of the earth might know
...d of the Lord is powerful
...lways fear the Lord your God.

Joshua 4:24

He did this so that all the peoples of the earth might know that the hand of the Lord is powerful and so that you might always fear the Lord your God.

Joshua 4:24

He did this so that all th...

He did this so that all the peoples of the earth might

that the hand of the Lord is po

and so that you might always fear the Lord your

Joshua 4:24